The Prodigal Son

Discovering the Fullness of Life in the Love of the Father

LIFEWAY PRESS®
NASHVILLE, TENNESSEE

Editorial Team

STUDENT MINISTRY PUBLISHING

BEN MANDRELL
President, LifeWay Christian Resources

BEN TRUEBLOOD
Director, Student Ministry

JOHN PAUL BASHAM
Manager, Student Ministry Publishing

KAREN DANIEL
Editorial Team Leader

DREW DIXON
Content Editor

MORGAN HAWK
Production Editor

AMY LYON
Graphic Designer

Published by LifeWay Press® • © 2019 Matt Carter

ISBN 978-1-5359-9639-6 • Item 005822494

Dewey decimal classification: 226.8
Subject headings: BIBLE—PARABLES / PRODIGAL SON (PARABLES) / CHRISTIAN LIFE)

Unless indicated otherwise, Scripture quotations are taken from the New American Standard Bible® (NASB), Copyright © 1960, 1962, 1963, 1968, 1971, 1972, 1973, 1975, 1977, 1995 by The Lockman Foundation. Used by permission. www.lockman.org.

Scripture quotations are from the ESV® Bible (The Holy Bible, English Standard Version®), copyright © 2001 by Crossway, a publishing ministry of Good News Publishers. Used by permission. All rights reserved.

Scripture quotations marked CSB have been taken from the Christian Standard Bible®, Copyright © 2017 by Holman Bible Publishers. Used by permission. Christian Standard Bible® and CSB® are federally registered trademarks of Holman Bible Publishers.

REAP Method used with permission © 2008, 2009, 2010, 2011, 2012, 2014, 2016, The Austin Stone Community Church

To order additional copies of this resource, write to LifeWay Resources Customer Service; One LifeWay Plaza; Nashville, TN 37234; fax 615-251-5933; call toll free 800-458-2772; order online at LifeWay.com; or email orderentry@lifeway.com.

Printed in the United States of America

Student Ministry Publishing • LifeWay Resources • One LifeWay Plaza • Nashville, TN 37234

Contents

MATT CARTER serves as the Pastor of Preaching and Vision at the Austin Stone Community Church in Austin, Texas, which has grown from a core team of 15 to over 8,000 attending each Sunday since he planted it in 2002. Matt has co-authored multiple books including a commentary on the Gospel of John in The Christ Centered Exposition Commentary series. Matt also co-authored a novel of historical fiction, *Steal Away Home,* which tells the real-life story of famed pastor Charles Spurgeon's unlikely friendship with former slave-turned-missionary, Thomas Johnson. Matt holds an M.Div. from Southwestern Seminary and a Doctorate in Expositional Preaching from Southeastern Seminary. He and his wife, Jennifer, have been married for over 20 years, and they have three children, John Daniel, Annie, and Samuel.

Being a Christian is hard. There, I said it.

Wait a minute Matt, Jesus said my burden is easy and my yoke is light. And you know what? That's true. When I'm fully submitted to Jesus and walking well with Him, that verse makes all the sense in the world. My problem is that I have a pretty good track record of not consistently walking well with Jesus. Not because of Him, but because of me. Maybe that's not you're story, but it's mine. Christianity is hard. Worth it, but hard.

As a pastor for over 20 years, I've been preaching the Bible for a long time—been reading it for even longer. And when it comes to my biblical heroes, the ones that I have found over the years that I love the most, I love not because of the good they've done, but because of how they've failed. Why? Because I can relate.

There's a guy in the Bible I definitely wouldn't call my hero, or really a hero at all, but can certainly relate to. People often refer to him as "the prodigal son." If you grew up in church you know the story, but if you didn't here's the short version. This young man asks his dad for his inheritance before the old man dies. His father grants his wish and the young man takes off to foreign land, then squanders his inheritance and is forced to come home and beg for his father's forgiveness. That's actually not how the story ends, but I don't want to get too far ahead of myself.

When I was younger, I couldn't relate to this guy. But now, years later, unfortunately I can relate to him more than I ever thought possible.

If you're a Christian that has it all figured out, this book is not for you. If you're a Christian that's never really failed, fallen, or struggled, there might be a better use of your time than reading these pages. But if like me you love the Lord, but at times throughout your life you find yourself weary and broken, bruised and battered—maybe even hanging on by a thread—then this book is for you. No matter how weary you are, or how far you've fallen, your Father's love for you is greater than your wildest imagination. I wrote this book partly as therapy for myself and partly as a guide for people like you. And hopefully, it will guide you back into the arms of a loving Dad ready to welcome you home, wipe you clean, and call you His beloved son or daughter.

How to Use

This Bible study book includes eight weeks of content for group and personal study.

GROUP SESSIONS

Regardless of what day of the week your group meets, each session begins with the group session. Each group session uses the following format to facilitate simple yet meaningful interaction among group members and with the truths of God's Word presented in this study.

START. This page includes questions to get the conversation started and to introduce the video teaching.

WATCH. Here we're provided space to take notes on the video teaching.

DISCUSS. This section includes questions and statements that guide students to respond to Matt Carter's video teaching and to explore relevant Bible passages.

PERSONAL STUDY

PERSONAL STUDY. Each session provides two personal Bible studies. Each personal study works through the Scriptures to deepen your understanding of the week's topic, including questions designed to help you understand the Bible and apply its teaching to your life.

BIBLE READING PLAN. Additionally, each week of personal study provides four guided Bible readings that allow you to read related passages from the Scripture and learn to study them on your own. Each reading follows the REAP method, outlined on the next page.

The REAP Method

Each session features four Bible reading exercises, using the REAP method.

READ

Read the passages for today's Bible reading. Read the passages with an open heart, asking the Holy Spirit to give you words of encouragement, direction, and correction (2 Tim. 3:16). Underline the verses that stand out to you.

EXAMINE

Spend some time reflecting and writing about what you've read. Write down one or two of the key verses that stand out as particularly important. Ask yourself these questions and write down your thoughts:

- What is going on in the passage?
- Who is writing and who is he writing to?
- When was the author writing?
- What are the circumstances that the author is addressing?
- Does the writer mention anything that might indicate his purpose or intent?
- How do you think the author wants his audience to respond?

APPLY

After examining the passage, apply the text to your own life. Ask yourself these questions:

- What is God saying to me through this passage?
- How will I live differently and see myself differently today because of what I read?
- What are the things in my life that need to change in light of this truth?

PRAY

Pray through the passage and your application, asking God to change your heart and your life based on the time you've spent in His Word.

WEEK 1

The Problem

START

Welcome to Week 1. Use these questions to get the conversation started.

A parable is a simple story used to make a point. Jesus often used parables to teach His followers what it means to know and follow Him. Over the next eight weeks we're going to examine what many people think is the greatest parable Jesus told: the parable of the prodigal son.

Name one of your favorite stories. Why is it one of your favorites?

What have you learned from this story?

Stories engage our imagination in a way that other kinds of teaching don't. They guide us to discover things we might not otherwise notice by inviting us to see the world anew through the perspective of its characters. The parable of the prodigal son offers the same opportunity. At first glance, you might be thinking that a nearly 2000-year-old story doesn't sound that exciting, but consider this: The story of the prodigal son has been giving people hope and opening their eyes to the unmatched love of God for nearly 2000 years. Studying this parable together is an invitation to see the world from another perspective, a better perspective than our limited one—the perspective of the Father. As we do so, we will not only discover the hope-filled future the Father has for us but also the transforming power of His love for us.

Ask someone to read Luke 15:11-24.

Pray and ask God to use our time together. After praying, watch the video teaching.

WATCH

Use this section to take notes as you watch the Week 1 video.

DISCUSS

After viewing the video, discuss the following questions with your group.

What are some examples of ways you or someone you know has tried to find a "better life"? What's wrong with seeking out such a life outside of our heavenly Father?

Why are we hesitant to follow Jesus? What do we feel as though we are missing out on if we fully commit to Jesus?

Read Matthew 13:44. Why is the reward of following Jesus worth what it might cost us?

Following Jesus will always cost you something. It might cost you popularity, relationships, or "success." The good news, however, is that the rewards for following Him outweigh the costs. When people encounter the life-giving, soul-changing love of Jesus, they turn their backs on the temptations of the world and they go all-in.

What keeps us from seeing Jesus as worth losing everything else to pursue? What changes when we finally see Jesus as our greatest treasure?

What's wrong with seeing Jesus as merely a part of our lives instead of our whole life? What do we miss out on when we think this way?

Reading a story like the prodigal son, it may be tempting to think, "I would never do that." But at some point, we all doubt the love of our Father. The temptation for the far country exists for all of us. If it doesn't right now, it will in the future. For some of us the far county comes in the form of attempting to fit Jesus into our already busy schedules and priorities. The problem with such an approach is that it misses Jesus' inherent value—He is worthy of all that we are and all that we have. This story helps us see that no matter how far we roam, the best life is found in the love of the Father.

Where do you see yourself in this parable? Why should the parable cultivate sympathy for people who have wandered away from faith in Jesus or never experienced it to begin with?

Why Do People Walk Away?

The problem at the heart of this study is the reality that an increasing number of people are coming to the dangerous and false conclusion that life is more fulfilling outside God's love. Why is that? What keeps people from following Jesus? Interestingly, Jesus answered this question with another parable earlier in Luke.

Read Luke 8:4-15.

> **What are the four types of soil and what do they represent?**

Jesus used parables to teach truth to His followers. Though this story is often called "the parable of the sower," the focus is not really on the sower but on the soil where the seeds fall. Each type of soil received the Word of God, and each responded differently. Looking at each soil helps us identify reasons people walk away.

No Faith in the First Place

> **What kept the seed that fell on the hard ground from taking root? Why should we have compassion toward the people represented here?**

Some walk away from Jesus without ever having faith in the first place. The initial batch of seed fell on the hard dirt along the path, and the birds snatched the seed away before it could take root. This soil represents the people we know who reject God. The devil has blinded them from seeing the goodness of God (See 2 Cor. 4:4.).

> **What is wrong with assuming that because someone shows up at church or participates in religious activities, they're committed to Jesus?**

The Appearance of Faith

No amount of going to church, attending youth group, or even going on mission trips makes someone a Christ follower. Without a genuine faith, people are like the seed on the rocky soil; there is an appearance of growth, but it can't be sustained because they never personally experienced the life-changing salvation of Christ.

How can you be sure that your faith is your own and not merely motivated by a desire to please your friends or family members?

Allure of the World and Shame of Failure

The third soil that Jesus mentioned is filled with thorns that grow and choke faith "with worries and riches and pleasures of this life" (v. 14). The allure of the world was stronger than their faith in Jesus, so they pursued worldly temptations instead of Him.

In your experience, what are the "thorns" that make people chase experiences and comforts of the world instead of Jesus? When do you feel this temptation yourself?

Perhaps one of the reasons Christianity is on the decline in the United States is that people simply come to the conclusion that following Christ means missing out on the best life has to offer. With the third soil, Jesus could also be describing those people who allow worry that their past or current sins might keep them from Jesus.

Lack of Committed Christians

The fourth soil that Jesus described was the one where the Word of God was received with joy and began to produce fruit. This is what it means to follow Jesus—you find joy and contentment in Him and live to tell others about Him.

How would you describe your relationship with Jesus? Where do you need to grow?

The fourth soil—the committed Christian—produced an abundance of fruit. Maybe you don't know a fully committed Christian, but that doesn't mean you can't become one. The Bible screams from the rooftops that the greatest and fullest experience of happiness and blessing is found in only one place, and that is in a full-hearted, both feet planted, total life commitment to Jesus.

End your time today praying that God would help you commit to Him fully. Consider also taking some time to pray for people close to you who either don't know Jesus or have walked away from Him.

The Solution

Many people are asking serious questions about what it means to follow Jesus. They want to know, "If I follow Christ, what will it cost me? Will I miss out on life's best?"

The answer is a resounding "no." The only life worth having is found in knowing God the Father through His Son Jesus Christ. This is the central claim of Christianity. However, we need to realize these questions are not new; people have been asking them for centuries. Today we're going to look at one such question in John's Gospel.

A Bold Claim

Read John 6:53-58.

Jesus did not literally mean that people should eat His flesh or drink His blood. What did He mean? Why did the crowd find this statement offensive?

At this point, huge crowds followed Jesus wherever He went. He was working miracles, feeding the hungry, and healing the sick. Jesus paused, looked at the crowd and said that unless the crowd ate his flesh and drank His blood they could not follow Him (v. 53). By "flesh and blood," Jesus was referring to His whole being. Jesus was saying that unless they devoted themselves entirely to Him they could not find life.

Why is the claim Jesus made still shocking? Why do some find it offensive?

Jesus' claim that true life can only be found in Him is the most shocking and controversial claim in all the world. And Jesus made this claim repeatedly. It offended people in the first century and it offends people today. The huge crowd following Jesus—drawn in by His teaching and miracles—didn't understand. Many of them turned and walked away. His disciples were standing with their mouths wide open, stunned that the popularity of their leader had just plummeted, but Jesus was unmoved by it.

A Bold Response

Peter realized life is found in only one place—Jesus.

Read John 6:66-69.

What does Peter's confession in verse 68 tell us about Jesus? About us?

All people are hardwired to pursue a life of purpose and meaning because we were all created to relate to God. Jesus made a bold claim when He said that the fullness of life can only be found in following Him completely. In other words, if we are looking for life outside of Jesus we will never find it.

Peter asked Jesus, "Lord, to whom shall we go?" Think for a moment about your friends who don't know God. Where do they turn to find life? What are the results?

We live in a culture where people are desperate for a different way to live. No amount of friends, trophies, awards, money, or social media followers can give us the life we desperately desire. These things may make us feel good for a moment, but they can't ultimately satisfy us.

Those of us who know Jesus have a responsibility to show other people the way to abundant life (John 10:10). How will the people around us see a better way if we aren't willing to show them? How are we going to turn the tide of death and despair in our culture if Christians live no differently?

How does the way you live show people what it means to follow Jesus?

This world desperately needs to be shown a new way. The world needs ordinary people who decide to go all-in when it comes to following Christ. Our culture is desperate for a generation of believers that don't just make Jesus a part of their lives, but passionately put Him first and show this world with their everyday lives that yes, there is a better path—a path of peace and love and joy and purpose.

What might you need to let go of to follow Jesus more closely? Is there anything you need to give up?

How could you point a friend to the hope and life that is found in Jesus this week?

Pray that God will help you find life in Jesus alone. Use Psalm 16:11 as a guide.

Luke 15:11-24

Further familiarize yourself with the story we will be diving into over these next eight weeks together.

- -

Read

Read the passage slowly and carefully with an open heart, asking the Holy Spirit to direct, encourage, and correct you as you read.

- -

Examine

Pick a few verses and look at them more closely to gain a deeper understanding of what the Bible is saying.

- -

Apply

Consider how you will live differently in light of what you read.

- How are you like the younger son?
- Jot down one way you will remind yourself this week of God's love for you.

- -

Pray

Pray through the passage and your application, asking God to change your heart and to change your life based on the time you've spent in His Word.

Matthew 13:44-46

Jesus told a series of brief parables to explain the true value of the kingdom of heaven. Nothing in life can give us what Christ's kingdom offers.

Read

Read the passage slowly and carefully with an open heart, asking the Holy Spirit to direct, encourage, and correct you as you read.

Examine

Pick a few verses and look at them more closely to gain a deeper understanding of what the Bible is saying.

Apply

Consider how you will live differently in light of what you read.

- Jot down a list of things you treasure or greatly value.
- Circle any of the things on your list that might be hindering you from loving Jesus more.

Pray

Pray through the passage and your application, asking God to change your heart and to change your life based on the time you've spent in His Word.

Psalm 16:1-11

True and lasting pleasure is only found in the presence of God.

Read

Read the passage slowly and carefully with an open heart, asking the Holy Spirit to give you words of encouragement, direction, and correction.

Examine

Pick a few verses and look at them more closely to gain a deeper understanding of what the Bible is saying.

Apply

Consider how you will live differently in light of what you read.

- Make a list of some of the most common things teens today want out of life. Circle those that most appeal to you.
- How well do these things line up with the joy God desires for you to experience through your relationship with Him?

Pray

Pray through the passage and your application, asking God to change your heart and to change your life based on the time you've spent in His Word.

Hebrews 3:12-19

The author of Hebrews provides a sobering warning about the deceitfulness of sin and its desire to lead into false beliefs.

Read

Read the passage slowly and carefully with an open heart, asking the Holy Spirit to give you words of encouragement, direction, and correction.

Examine

Pick a few verses and look at them more closely to gain a deeper understanding of what the Bible is saying.

Apply

Consider how you will live differently in light of what you read.

- What are some specific ways you might need to "watch out" that you don't develop an "unbelieving heart" (Heb. 13:12)?
- How might you encourage someone in their faith this week?

Pray

Pray through the passage and your application, asking God to change your heart and to change your life based on the time you've spent in His Word.

WEEK 2

The Lie

START

Welcome to Week 2. Use these questions to get the conversation started.

In week 1 of the personal study we addressed several reasons people wander away from God. Which of these do you think is most common?

Last week we looked at the central question in the story of the prodigal son.

Are we missing out on life's best by following Christ?

Looking at the world around us, it's clear that scores of people believe that the best life is found in doing your own thing and going your own way. When we choose to elevate ourselves, we are rejecting God. This is what the Bible calls sin.

As followers of Jesus, we know sin never delivers on what it promises. So what leads people to sin in the first place? The Bible has the answer.

One of the amazing things about Scripture is that although it was written 2000 years ago, its truths are timeless and the Bible remains 100 percent accurate. God knew His children would face a world where they would question whether or not following Him was the best choice. This week we will focus on the lie that led the prodigal (and us) to wander from home.

Without naming names, share a time when someone lied to you. What made this lie painful?

Ask someone to read Luke 15:11-12.

Pray and ask God to use our time together.
After praying, watch the video teaching.

WATCH

Use this section to take notes as you watch the Week 2 video.

DISCUSS

After viewing the video, discuss the following questions with your group.

What's shocking about the request the younger son made to his father? What was the younger son saying about his father by making this request?

How does what we believe impact what we do? When have you ever made a bad decision based on a wrong belief?

The younger son's request was bold and cruel. He was basically saying, "Dad, I wish you were dead. I'd rather have your money than you." For him to make this request, the son had to believe life in the far country was better than life in his father's house. Similarly, when we chase after sin, it's because we have believed the lie that disobeying God will be good for us. In this week's teaching, Matt said there were two primary reasons we believe lies: our sinful nature and the devil.

If we know sin is wrong, why does sin always seem like a good idea at the time? How does our sinful nature affect our choices?

Read John 8:44. How did Jesus describe the devil? Why is it helpful to know who the devil is and how he operates?

Observing the world around us, what lies are the people around you most susceptible to believe?

What are some ways we can see through the lies? How might we redirect our focus to the life that is only available through faith in Jesus Christ?

The Origin of the Lie

Our culture is obsessed with superhero movies. We can't get enough of them. Part of what makes these movies great is their beginnings, where we are introduced to the hero's powers but also to their flaws.

Most of us don't have superpowers—we can't throw a car with ease or swing from webs by our finger tips. However, we do all have a fatal flaw; we're all sinners. Every one of us has exchanged the truth of God for a lie (Rom. 1:25). Accepting the lie of sin and acting on it brings death and misery. Thankfully, the Bible shows us where sin came from and how to overcome it. We're going to tackle those two ideas this week. Today, we will look at sin's origin, and next time, we will see how to overcome its influence. The Bible teaches that we buy into the lie of sin for two primary reasons—our sinful nature and the lies of the devil.

In this week's video teaching we heard from Jesus concerning the devil:

> *He was a murderer from the beginning, and does not stand in the truth because there is no truth in him. Whenever he speaks a lie, he speaks from his own nature, for he is a liar and the father of lies.*
> **JOHN 8:44**

How is Jesus' description of Satan different from the cartoon version our culture asks us to believe? Why is this difference important for us to acknowledge?

Scripture describes the devil as a roaring lion (1 Pet. 5:8), cunning (2 Cor. 11:3), and powerful (Jude 9). But before the Bible tells us this, we see the original story of sin in the opening pages of the Bible. In fact, Satan tells the very first lie.

The First Lie

Read Genesis 3:1-7.

What lie did Satan ask Adam and Eve to believe? How did Satan's empty promises fail Adam and Eve? What were the results?

Satan's tactics are deceptive, but they aren't new. Satan slithered up to them, and dropped an outright lie. He said, "If you eat from the fruit, you will not surely die."

Instead, he promised that eating the fruit would bring life. They believed the lie, disobeyed God, and death entered the story of humanity.

Consider your own life. What lies do we usually believe when we fall into sin?

Satan is not stupid. He's quite the opposite—he's brilliant. And though he knows there will come a day when he will be destroyed forever, until then, he's going to inflict as much damage as he can. He will lie to you just as he did Adam and Eve. Believing his lies only brings pain and death. Romans 1 paints a vivid picture of what happens in our lives when we embrace the lie of sin.

The Effects of the Lie

Read Romans 1:25-32.

According to the Scriptures, what happens when we exchange the truth about God for a lie? Who are we really worshiping when we do this?

Romans 1 puts a mirror to our own experience. These verses restate what we will see in the parable of the prodigal son. Satan isn't mentioned in the parable, but if you listen closely you can hear the whisper of the father of lies in the young man's ear: "Hey, you're really missing out by living with your dad. Don't you think life would be more fulfilling if you lived by your own rules? Do you see that big city over there? That's where *real* life is happening." Every day we are tempted, just like the young man in our story, to exchange the truth about our heavenly Father for a lie.

Read 1 John 1:9. What hope is there for those of us who have embraced a lie?

End your time by meditating on this truth—though we are attacked by the father of lies everyday, one simple truth can undo all the effects of his lies. We're going to look at this more closely in our next day of study.

The Truth

When you were in preschool, you learned opposites. Up and down. Inside and outside. Loud and quiet. You might feel a bit silly reading simple ideas from a toddler's book. However, if you remember those days, you know one of the first moral ideas you learned as a child is that the opposite of a lie is the truth.

Sin is such a pervasive problem that we often can't see the simple solution for the ongoing sin in our life. Lies can be overcome with the truth. In order to combat the lies of the devil, we must believe the truth about God. Today we're going to look at two examples from the Bible to illustrate this point.

Exceptional Belief

Read Matthew 8:5-13.

> **What did Jesus find surprising about the Roman soldier's faith? Why does this kind of faith seem rare?**

Notice what happened—the soldier simply believed Jesus. He believed that if Jesus said the words, it was going to happen. This is incredible considering the Roman soldier wasn't taught about God growing up. God is honored when His people believe Him. It's the simplest definition of a word that is used all the time in Scripture. It's called faith. Faith means trusting what God says.

> **In what area in your life do you simply need to believe what God says? Jot down a prayer asking God to help you trust Him in that area.**

Believe in Me Also

If you ever find yourself doubting what God has said, you are not alone. Jesus' disciples did this often. Thomas needed to see Jesus' hands (John 20:25). Peter denied Christ three times (John 18:27). Sometimes when Jesus' disciples doubted him, He rebuked them, but just as often He comforted them.

Read John 14:1-6.

> **What reason did Jesus give for His disciples to trust Him?**

Compare what Jesus says about Himself in John 14:6 with what He said about Satan a few chapters earlier in John 8:44.

Why is it good news to us that Jesus comforted His disciples?

Thinking about what it means to embrace the truth, we have to acknowledge we often fail. One of the blessings of studying the story of the prodigal son is it gives us the chance to consider the ways the prodigal failed without failing ourselves.

Satan is an expert at deception. But even when we take the bait, God's Word is still true. This Bible study exists in part because of a sincere belief that in order to resist the lies we need to constantly be filling ourselves with truth.

Finding Truth

Read 2 Timothy 3:16-17.

What did Paul say the Bible is able to do for us? How does it help us combat the lies of the devil?

If you read the Bible regularly, what difference do you notice in your life when you spend time in God's Word compared to when you don't?

God gave us the Bible to lead us into truth. John 14 teaches us that truth is a person and His name is Jesus. For those of us who, like the prodigal, are tempted to wander from our Father's house, Jesus is telling us that we have a place in His Father's house if we place our faith in Him. He will show us the way as we rely on Him and daily seek His guidance in the Scriptures.

End your time by reading Psalm 119:105. Pray that God will use this study and more importantly His Word to lead you to His truth.

Don't forget to complete the four daily Bible readings before Week 3.

Genesis 3:1-24

Sin entered the world when Adam and Eve chose to believe a lie about God's character and nature. We lie to ourselves when we embrace sin.

Read

Read the passage slowly and carefully with an open heart, asking the Holy Spirit to give you words of encouragement, direction, and correction.

Examine

Pick a few verses and look at them more closely to gain a deeper understanding of what the Bible is saying.

Apply

Consider how you will live differently in light of what you read.

- What lie of Satan did Adam and Eve believe?
- How is Satan currently lying to you? Jot down a truth you learned this week to combat this lie.

Pray

Pray through the passage and your application, asking God to change your heart and to change your life based on the time you've spent in His Word.

Romans 5:1-21

All human beings are broken by sin and as a result are under the curse of death. But even though our sin is great, the grace of Jesus is bigger.

Read

Read the passage slowly and carefully with an open heart, asking the Holy Spirit to give you words of encouragement, direction, and correction.

Examine

Pick a few verses and look at them more closely to gain a deeper understanding of what the Bible is saying.

Apply

Consider how you will live differently in light of what you read.

- Create a list comparing the results of sin with the results of God's grace in Christ.

Pray

Pray through the passage and your application, asking God to change your heart and to change your life based on the time you've spent in His Word.

Romans 1:18-28

Spend time together truly contemplating the effects of sin.

Read

Read the passage slowly and carefully with an open heart, asking the Holy Spirit to give you words of encouragement, direction, and correction.

Examine

Pick a few verses and look at them more closely to gain a deeper understanding of what the Bible is saying.

Apply

Consider how you will live differently in light of what you read.

- Which of the sinful attitudes and actions Paul mentions in Romans 1:18-28 most tempts you? How will you combat this temptation this week?

Pray

Pray through the passage and your application, asking God to change your heart and to change your life based on the time you've spent in His Word.

Ephesians 2:1-10

Sin is serious and its effects are widespread, but all who turn to Jesus in repentance and faith can find freedom from slavery to sin.

Read

Read the passage slowly and carefully with an open heart, asking the Holy Spirit to give you words of encouragement, direction, and correction.

Examine

Pick a few verses and look at them more closely to gain a deeper understanding of what the Bible is saying.

Apply

Consider how you will live differently in light of what you read.

- Make a list comparing and contrasting who you were before coming to faith in Christ (Eph. 2:1-3) and how Paul describes you in Christ (Eph. 2:4-10).

Pray

Pray through the passage and your application, asking God to change your heart and to change your life based on the time you've spent in His Word.

WEEK 3

The Step

START

Last week we took a deeper look into the lie that our best life is found outside the love of our heavenly Father. What was the most helpful takeaway from your personal study?

Our biggest missteps don't happen all at once; they're usually the result of a series of bad decisions. Take lying to your parents, for example. Before you tell a lie, you have to determine there is some truth worth covering. Thinking about lying isn't wrong—lying is. To tell a lie requires a previous step.

Every sin has a beginning. On the front end, sin always looks enticing, fun, satisfying, and enjoyable. But sin will always take you to places you never intended to go. Last week, we considered the origin of sin. This week, we will look at what happens when we take the next step and give into sin.

Share about a time when you broke your parents' or caretakers' rules. Was there a process that led to your mistake or did it happen all at once?

Ask someone to read 2 Samuel 11:1-4.

Pray and ask God to use our time together.
After praying, watch the video teaching

WATCH

Use this section to take notes as you watch the Week 3 video.

DISCUSS

After viewing the video, discuss the following questions with your group.

The story of David and Bathsheba is not a fairytale that was told to make a point. It really happened. However, like the prodigal son, we can track the process of sin in David's life in the hope that we might avoid the same devastating choices.

How did David move rapidly from being tempted to giving into sin? What is an earlier step he could have taken to avoid giving in?

First, David was at home when he should've been at battle with his soldiers.

What are some ways that we put ourselves into situations where we are more likely to enter into sin?

Next, David saw a beautiful woman, Bathsheba, bathing across the way. Seeing an attractive woman is not a sin. But what happened next was—David asked who the woman was, discovered she was married, and still asked his men to go and get her. And, by the way, David was married too. David used his power to sleep with Bathsheba and have her husband murdered.

At what point did David step beyond temptation and into sin? What is the difference between temptation and sin?

Why is it beneficial to be aware of the things that most tempt us?

How does the lie of sin convince us that embracing temptation is worth the risk? If you are comfortable, share an example from your own life.

What are some things we could do to stop temptation before it gives birth to sin? How can we help each other here?

Anatomy of a Fall

So far we've talked about how the prodigal son became convinced there was a better life for him outside of the love of his father. But before we continue, let's take a closer look at what causes us to make the decision to walk away from our heavenly Father.

Temptation

Read James 1:12-15.

> **According to James, where does temptation come from? Where does it not come from? Why is this important to understand?**

> **James connects temptations to trials. How do our temptations often come out of our trials?**

We can't see inside the mind of the prodigal, so we can't know for certain what made him decide to walk away from his father's house. Jesus doesn't tell us. However, James teaches us that our temptations are often related to our trials. For instance, if you are experiencing financial difficulty, you might be tempted to steal. If you are lonely, you might struggle with seeking company in inappropriate relationships.

God, however, never tempts us. God is never at fault when we walk away from Him. While it's true that God tests us, He always does so to strengthen our faith, never to tempt us to sin. Sin is always our choice. We fall into sin because sin is enticing.

The Allure of Sin

Alluring isn't a word you hear very often. It means "powerfully and mysteriously attractive or fascinating; seductive."[1] James painted a picture of a fish attracted to a lure in the water, but the fish is unaware that the lure will kill it. Temptation becomes a problem when it entices us into sin, because just like the fish, when sin reels us in, death is always waiting at the other end of the line.

> **Why is it crucial for us to realize sin is alluring? What does it mean to be "carried away" or "enticed" by our own lust (v. 14)?**

---

1. "allure," *New Oxford American Dictionary*, 3rd ed. (Oxford University Press, 2010).

How has experience taught you that temptation is misleading and never delivers on its promise?

A fish wouldn't take the bait if it realized the inevitable outcome. When Christians embrace temptation, they have forgotten that sin leads to death. God is the only One who can deliver on every promise, and He does every time. We've already seen that God doesn't tempt us; now let's look at what God does.

Grace in Temptation

Read James 1:16-18

James contrasts the emptiness of temptation with the goodness of God. When Satan tempts us, he is hoping that we believe the lie that embracing temptation leads to blessing. But temptation is always a bait and switch. James tells us every good thing comes from God. Sin always brings death (Rom. 6:23) and God always brings life—the kind of full and meaningful life that is worth having. With Jesus there is no trick, but only grace, love, and life. Jesus delivers on every promise.

How did James refer to the people he was writing to in verse 16?

In verse 16, James addresses the church. In fact, the entire New Testament was written to the church—a group of people seeking to follow Jesus together. Sin isolates us from God and from other people. And that is exactly what Satan wants. God intends for His children to live in community with other believers. We're meant to fight our temptations together. Imagine what might have been different for the prodigal if he had a wise friend able to provide good advice.

Look up James 5:16. Why should we desire the kind of relationships where we can share our struggles and sins with one another?

End your time today being honest about your temptations. List them below. Ask God to deliver you, knowing that He has the strength and power to do so. Then make time to talk to someone you can trust about your struggles.

David's Great Sin(s)?

In the previous personal study, we saw how temptation invites us to take a first step into sin which will lead us into struggle, misery, and ultimately death. Today we're going to turn our attention to the life of David and the consequences of his sin.

Taking the Leap

Slowly read 2 Samuel 11:1-27 and then answer the following questions.

Where in this passage do we see David being tempted? At what points did David's temptations turn into sin? How did his sin lead to more sin?

At what points could David have resisted these temptations?

Initially, David remained at home while his men engaged in battle. David wasn't where he should've been, and this created the opportunity for David to see Bathsheba on a nearby rooftop. At this point, David's life spiraled into a cycle of temptation and sin. From lust to adultery to deceit and murder—David's life slipped further and further off track. This series of events defined the rest of David's life, and he was confronted with a variety of consequences. The kingdom David ruled was plagued with wars and betrayed by family. (See 2 Sam. 15–19.) David's life never quite returned to what it was before that night on the rooftop.

Imagine if the elderly David could speak to the younger David that night on the roof. What do you think he would say?

Before sinning, we often believe the lie that what we're considering is "no big deal." How does this episode demonstrate there is no such thing as a small sin?

If David could go back in time and speak to his younger self he would surely grab that young man by the shoulders, pull him close, and plead with him to go home alone. He would warn that the momentary pleasure David is seeking would set into motion a series of events he could never recover from. He would tell the young David that every step into sin is really a leap into death. Death of purity, death of integrity, death of trust, death of the abundant life that God has promised.

Looking Inward

If you know Jesus, you never read Scripture alone; the Holy Spirit is present with you, guiding you into all truth (John 16:13). Because of this reality, when we read David's account, we're not just reading about the sin in David's life, we're also being confronted with the presence of sin in our own life.

The point of this next exercise is not to reopen old wounds or introduce fresh shame, but to help you see that David's experience with sin and temptation isn't an isolated incident. Instead, it's an example we can learn from that points us to Jesus (1 Cor. 10:11).

Identify a past sin in your own life. What temptation(s) did you experience before succumbing to this sin? What lie did you believe that led you to think it was a good idea?

How did that sin fail to deliver on its promises?

If you could go back and talk to your previous self before you committed the sin, what would you say? What lessons from David's story can you apply to your situation?

The goal of asking ourselves painful questions like these is to shine a light into our own darkness. If you keep reading in 2 Samuel, you will find that David was confronted about his sin by the prophet Nathan (2 Sam. 12). It took some encouragement, but David admitted his fault and sought restoration (Ps. 51).

Maybe this exercise hit a little close to home and you are standing at that same crossroads where David and the prodigal stood—the crossroads of temptation and sin. Ignore the lying whispers of your enemy and choose to believe the words of your Savior. There is no future or abundant life to be found on the rooftop across the way or in a far away land. Stay at home.

End your time today by searching your own heart. Ask God to reveal any sin you need to repent from and commit to refusing to fight sin alone.

Don't forget to complete the four days of daily Bible readings before the next session.

2 Samuel 12:1-15

After David sinned with Bathsheba, God sent the prophet Nathan to confront and rebuke David.

Read

Read the passage slowly and carefully with an open heart, asking the Holy Spirit to give you words of encouragement, direction, and correction.

Examine

Pick a few verses and look at them more closely to gain a deeper understanding of what the Bible is saying.

Apply

Consider how you will live differently in light of what you read.

- When you face a situation like David, where you find yourself alone with plenty of time to think about a particular temptation, how will you respond? How might you protect yourself now from making horrible decisions in the future?

Pray

Pray through the passage and your application, asking God to change your heart and to change your life based on the time you've spent in His Word.

2 Samuel 12:16-31

David responded to Nathan's correction with genuine sorrow and mourning as he felt the weight of his sin.

Read

Read the passage slowly and carefully with an open heart, asking the Holy Spirit to give you words of encouragement, direction, and correction.

Examine

Pick a few verses and look at them more closely to gain a deeper understanding of what the Bible is saying.

Apply

Consider how you will live differently in light of what you read.

- How could you guard yourself against sexual sin? Jot down a list of practical steps you could take.

Pray

Pray through the passage and your application, asking God to change your heart and to change your life based on the time you've spent in His Word.

Proverbs 2:1-22

Avoiding sin requires wisdom which can be gained from God's Word. In this chapter, Solomon compared sin to an adulterous woman.

Read

Read the passage slowly and carefully with an open heart, asking the Holy Spirit to give you words of encouragement, direction, and correction.

Examine

Pick a few verses and look at them more closely to gain a deeper understanding of what the Bible is saying.

Apply

Consider how you will live differently in light of what you read.

- There is more to fighting sin than just not doing certain things—it requires finding better things to do that would honor God and serve others. What is one better thing you will do this week?

Pray

Pray through the passage and your application, asking God to change your heart and to change your life based on the time you've spent in His Word.

Proverbs 4:1-27

Solomon gave wisdom in the form of advice from a father to a son.

Read

Read the passage slowly and carefully with an open heart, asking the Holy Spirit to give you words of encouragement, direction, and correction.

Examine

Pick a few verses and look at them more closely to gain a deeper understanding of what the Bible is saying.

Apply

Consider how you will live differently in light of what you read.

- Compare the two ways to live that Solomon shares. What is one step you could take this week toward choosing the better path?

Pray

Pray through the passage and your application, asking God to change your heart and to change your life based on the time you've spent in His Word.

WEEK 4

The Consequences

START

Welcome to Week 4. Use these questions to get the conversation started.

Last week we looked at what happened as King David fell into sin. How was looking at David's life helpful in fighting the temptations you face?

No one would choose to do something wrong if they knew they would be caught and punished. The prodigal would have never asked his father for his inheritance if he understood the consequences that awaited him on his journey. Before he requested his inheritance, he noticed the far county. To the younger son, the far country beamed with the promises of a better life.

A couple weeks ago, we watched as the prodigal took that fateful first step down the path toward sin and rebellion in a distant land. This week we're going to take a look at what he found waiting for him at the end of the road. This session is about the consequences of our sin and rebellion.

What is the most memorable or humorous punishment you received when you were younger?

Ask someone to read Luke 15:13-16.

Pray and ask God to use our time together.
After praying, watch the video teaching.

WATCH

Use this section to take notes as you watch the Week 4 video.

DISCUSS

After viewing the video, discuss the following questions with your group.

Why does it often take us going our own way before we realize the danger of our actions? What keeps us from listening to warnings along the way?

Jesus wasted no time revealing the consequences of the prodigal's decision. The young man took his father's gift and wasted it on "loose living." The language here communicates that the man took all he was given and spent it without giving much thought to his actions. He was broke and unfulfilled.

When have you wasted your money, time, or energy on something you thought would make you happy? Why did the thing you spent your money on disappoint you?

What are some ways we seek the far country today?

When we pursue the far country, what is it that we're really wanting? Why does sin always leave us feeling empty?

Matt taught that Ecclesiastes 3:11 gives us a clue into what the prodigal (and we) hoped to find in the far country. All of us are searching for fulfillment that can only be found in God. Sin will always leave us broken and unfulfilled.

Read Ecclesiastes 3:11 together.

How have you observed this verse to be true in your experience? How does this verse point us forward to Jesus?

What are some ways people today try to find happiness and fulfillment? Is it possible to find happiness and fulfillment apart from Christ? Explain.

How can we root our happiness in Jesus? How might we help other people identify their longing for eternity and their need for Jesus?

The Beautiful Mirage of Excess

*[God] has made everything appropriate in its time. He has also set
eternity in their heart, yet so that man will not find out the work
which God has done from the beginning even to the end.*
ECCLESIASTES 3:11

When you hear the word "eternity," what comes to mind? What does your desire to live for eternity tell you about yourself?

God hardwired all of us to long for eternity because He wants us to find life in Him. God determines where we live, what we do, and who we know, in order that we might follow the evidence back to the eternal source (Acts 17:24-28). In His grace, God has placed signs all around us that point to Him—the Maker. However, the prodigal son shows us a problem we all face. All of us pursue the signs and miss the Maker. The Book of Ecclesiastes tackles this problem head on.

The Emptiness of Success

Read Ecclesiastes 2:1-11.

What did Solomon seek in hopes that it would fulfill him? How does Solomon's list compare with the things people seek today?

What was the result of Solomon's efforts to find fulfillment (v. 11)?

After David died, God chose David's son, Solomon, to rule in his place. As great as David was, Solomon was greater. He was the wisest man who ever lived and one of the wealthiest. Under his leadership, Israel expanded and prospered. He had it all, but all that he had blinded him from seeing what really mattered. His desire, wealth, power, and pleasure robbed his heart from God, and all his wealth left him empty.

Most scholars believe that Solomon wrote Ecclesiastes near the end of his life when he found, like the prodigal, that the best and most fulfilling life is not found in what our culture prizes. The whole point of the Book of Ecclesiastes is the claim that *nothing* in all the world can meet and satisfy the deepest longings of the human heart. The best the world has to offer can never produce in us the happiness our hearts long for, because that type of happiness can only come from God. Like the prodigal, Solomon came by this wisdom the hard way.

The Most Miserable Person in the World

Read 1 Kings 11:1-13 and compare it with Luke 15:13-16.

> What consequences did Solomon and the prodigal suffer by pursuing the best they thought life had to offer?

> Though you may not have failed as publicly as Solomon and the prodigal, when have you felt the consequences of pursuing sin over God?

Though all people are hardwired with eternity in their hearts, not all people search for eternity in a way that they can find it. Those who don't know God do this all the time. But what happens when a Christian searches for fulfillment apart from God? I want to answer with a bold claim:

*A Christian who is walking in unrepentant sin is
the most miserable person in the world.*

Obviously, this is a huge generalization—and to be clear, when someone who doesn't know God pursues sin, it definitely leads to misery. But the effects of sin on a believer are more consequential because their hearts have found the true source of contentment. They have traced the desire for eternity back to the source.

Read John 17:3

Jesus is telling us that our longing for eternity is satisfied in Him and Him alone. When a Christian tries to replace his or her heart's desire—Jesus—with anything else, it will always result in misery. Our longing for eternity can never be satisfied with anything other than Jesus. He is the only path to everlasting life.

> Are you currently seeking purpose and meaning in anything other than a relationship with Jesus? If so, where?

> End your time today thanking God for the hope and joy He has given you in Christ. Ask that He would help you pursue Him above all else.

True Blessing

Blessing According to Culture

What would you say is your greatest blessing? Why?

If you didn't know, Kevin Durant is one of the most successful basketball players in NBA history. He has won two championships, one league MVP, been to the all-star game ten times, was Rookie of the Year, and has won two Olympic gold medals. Durant is consistently at the top of the league in jersey sales and has a contract with Nike for tens of millions of dollars. From the outside looking in, Durant seems like a guy who has it all.

Yet after Durant won his first championship, he didn't find it fulfilling.[1] Durant had dreamed of hoisting the Larry O'Brien trophy his whole life, so why did the experience not live up to the dream? Durant discovered championships aren't enough; we are designed for more. True blessing cannot be found in earthly accomplishments. No achievement, enjoyment, or praise will ever make us feel complete. The best life is found by pursuing the life God desires for us. If that's true, what does that life look like?

Jesus described the life God desires for us in His most famous teaching, known as the Sermon on the Mount. Jesus began with a series of brief statements, called the Beatitudes, about what it means to be blessed.

Blessing According to Jesus

Read Matthew 5:1-12.

What did Jesus mean when He used the word "blessed"?

Make a list of what Jesus said is a blessed life. Which of these is most surprising?

How does Jesus' list of those who are blessed compare with our culture's values?

The specific Greek word in Matthew 5:1-12 used for "blessed" carries with it the idea of the fullest expression of happiness a person can experience. The first Beatitude (v. 3) and the sixth (v. 10) have the same reward—"theirs is the kingdom of heaven."

1. Marcel Mutoni, "Steve Nash: Kevin Durant 'Not Fulfilled' After First Warriors Chamionship," *SLAM* [online], 3 July 2019. Available from the Internet: https://www.slamonline.com/nba/steve-nash-kevin-durant-not-fulfilled-after-first-warriors-championship/.

According to Jesus, blessing is found when we are poor in spirit, mourning, gentle, desiring righteousness, merciful, pursing purity, making peace, and even when we are being persecuted and insulted. Let's take a closer look at what Jesus counts as a blessed life.

What does it mean to be "poor in spirit" (v. 3)? How is this different from the way the prodigal (and most of us) live?

Many people believe that we are happiest when we "follow our heart." How does this compare with Jesus' teaching to be "pure in heart" (v. 8)?

To be poor in spirit means to be humble before God, recognizing that we are entirely dependent upon Him. We are poor in spirit when we agree with God about our sin, turn to Him for grace, and allow Him to purify our hearts. The word "pure" in verse 8 means unmixed or undivided. So what Jesus is conveying is that a Christian can experience the greatest level of happiness when his or her heart is fully devoted to God and not divided by God and something else. So if the fullness of joy is found in God's presence, a divided heart will prevent you from experiencing that fullness.

How can God use your painful lessons in life to help you grow?

Sin keeps you from meeting the deepest longings of your heart, because those longings can only be fulfilled in Jesus. Walking in sin will produce emptiness and misery every single time. But the good news is that when a believer sins, that emptiness and misery will always serve as a reminder that there is a place, and a home, and a Person that will always take you back, restore you, and truly fill you.

You might be in that place today. If that's you, I want you to know that the emptiness you feel as a result of your sin is the kindness of God gently calling you home. Make no mistake, sin and its consequences are profound. But even in the midst of your sin God is still at work. Sin's inability to satisfy your deepest longings is nothing more than the tender and beautiful whisper of God that there's more to this life than what you're experiencing. Ask God to help you see sin for what it is—vanity—and I promise you He will.

End your time today confessing the ways you have pursued your own path at the expense of God's best in your life. If God is convicting you of sin, thank Him for pulling you back and leading you to find life in Him. And don't forget to complete the four days of Bible readings before Week 5.

REAP

Luke 15:11-24

At the halfway mark of our study, take another look at the prodigal son.

Read

Read the passage slowly and carefully with an open heart, asking the Holy Spirit to give you words of encouragement, direction, and correction.

Examine

Pick a few verses and look at them more closely to gain a deeper understanding of what the Bible is saying.

Apply

Consider how you will live differently in light of what you read.

- The prodigal son was confronted with the consequences of his own sin. How have you been tempted to sin lately?
- What is alluring about that sin? What might some of the consequences be if you gave in to this temptation?

Pray

Pray through the passage and your application, asking God to change your heart and to change your life based on the time you've spent in His Word.

Romans 6:20-23

Paul highlights the consequences of sin against the gift of grace.

Read

Read the passage slowly and carefully with an open heart, asking the Holy Spirit to give you words of encouragement, direction, and correction.

Examine

Pick a few verses and look at them more closely to gain a deeper understanding of what the Bible is saying.

Apply

Consider how you will live differently in light of what you read.

- Have you ever felt stuck in a particular sin that you just couldn't seem to get out of? According to Paul in Romans 6:20-23 how can we be freed?
- Write a prayer to God thanking Him for offering you true freedom from sin.

Pray

Pray through the passage and your application, asking God to change your heart and to change your life based on the time you've spent in His Word.

Matthew 6:19-24

Many people abandon God to pursue worldly goods like money and stuff. Jesus warned about the consequences of this pursuit in the Sermon on the Mount.

Read

Read the passage slowly and carefully with an open heart, asking the Holy Spirit to give you words of encouragement, direction, and correction.

Examine

Pick a few verses and look at them more closely to gain a deeper understanding of what the Bible is saying.

Apply

Consider how you will live differently in light of what you read.

- Create a list of things you value. Circle the three that are most important to you.
- Ask God to reveal to you whether any of the things are coming before your relationship with Him. Pray that God would help you keep these things in proper perspective and to value Jesus above all.

Pray

Pray through the passage and your application, asking God to change your heart and to change your life based on the time you've spent in His Word.

Ephesians 4:30-32

Walking in sin grieves the Holy Spirit and keeps us from experiencing the fullness of life available to us in Christ.

Read

Read the passage slowly and carefully with an open heart, asking the Holy Spirit to give you words of encouragement, direction, and correction.

Examine

Pick a few verses and look at them more closely to gain a deeper understanding of what the Bible is saying.

Apply

Consider how you will live differently in light of what you read.

- How should Paul's teaching in Ephesians 4:30-32 shape the way you interact with others at school, in your activities, and on social media?

Pray

Pray through the passage and your application, asking God to change your heart and to change your life based on the time you've spent in His Word.

WEEK 5

The Realization

START

- -

Welcome to Week 5. Use these questions to get the conversation started.

Last week we talked about how God has put eternity in the hearts of men (Ecc. 3:11). As you've processed this over the last week, how have you observed the statement to be true?

In Week 4, we saw the prodigal at the end of his rope, broken, and tending to pigs. He learned that the lights of the far country were not as bright as he'd hoped. Everything he thought would bring him happiness had actually produced pain and misery he never could've imagined. The prodigal had a wake-up call and realized he should never have left his father in the first place.

This week we're going to take a look at what happens in the lives of Christians when they realize they are living in sin and disobedience. This realization is the first step on our journey back to the Father.

Describe a time when you were wrong about something? What made you realize you were wrong?

Ask someone to read Luke 15:17.

Pray and ask God to use our time together.
After praying, watch the video teaching..

The Realization   57

WATCH

Use this section to take notes as you watch the Week 5 video.

DISCUSS

After viewing the video, discuss the following questions with your group.

Last week we talked about the consequences of our sin. How does feeling the weight of our sins lead us to turn back to the Father?

When have you had a similar realization, like the prodigal, that your sin wasn't worth it?

Read Philippians 1:6. Why should this verse give wandering Christians the confidence to return to the Father?

Read John 16:7-8. How does the Holy Spirit help us realize the foolishness of our sin?

If you know Jesus and are wandering in the far off country of sin, the good news is that you will always come to your senses. God cares too much about His work in your life to let you continue in sin. When we are tempted to sin, the Spirit of God convicts and urges us toward reconciliation with our Father.

Matt ended our time by addressing two groups—those considering sin and those stuck in a pattern of sin. Let's end our time considering these groups together.

If you're in the first group, Matt mentioned that, for a believer, sin is a "monumental waste of time." What did he mean by this?

What does sin often cost us in terms of relationships, friendships, time, or energy? How might we remind ourselves of the cost before giving into temptation?

How might we help one another count the cost of sin and turn away from it when experiencing temptation?

God's Pursuit through Our Sin

What's the most helpful truth you've learned so far on our walk with the prodigal?

A Valid Question

This week we've crossed the halfway point. Here, our friend finds himself in a pigpen. The young man has fallen as far as a person can fall. He's abandoned his family, spent all of his inheritance on parties and prostitutes, and now finds himself in the worst situation of his life. A famine has come into the "far away land," and he finds himself starving, dirty, broke, and filled with shame. In that moment, he comes to his senses.

Read Luke 15:17

Have you ever wondered why God allows His children to sin in the first place? God is all-knowing and all-powerful, right? At any point, when his sons and daughters are standing at the crossroads of temptation and sin, He could intervene. But as we saw in a previous week, sometimes it takes us tasting the bitter fruit of sin for us to fully realize the sweetness of God's love.

Have you ever found yourself asking a similar question? How did you navigate the tension?

God's Work Through the Pigpen

Have you ever had a moment like the prodigal when you realized the sin you were pursing wasn't delivering on its promises? If you haven't yet, you probably will. And yet, God is still at work. When it comes to His sons and daughters, while God may let us take a trip to the far away land, He never lets us stay there—not forever (1 John 2:3-4). The apostle Paul wrote about this special grace of God in the midst of sin:

I am sure of this, that he who started a good work in you will carry it on to completion until the day of Christ Jesus.
PHILIPPIANS 1:6 (CSB)

Restate this verse in your own words.

Do you find it reassuring to know that God is always working in you and will not abandon you? Explain.

The church at Philippi was enduring a great deal of hardship from the culture around them. Unlike the prodigal, it was outside of their control. In their struggle, Paul reassured them that no matter what, God would not stop working among them. He would take the good work going on in their lives and bring it to completion.

Why is this promise important for us to remember when we mess up?

What happens when we mistakenly believe that God's love is circumstantial like our love for one another is?

God is not like us, and that's a good thing. No matter what happens, God is always with us. He will never leave us or forsake us (Heb. 13:5). If you are in a relationship with Jesus, He will never stop working in your life. He doesn't give up, as we might, when the road is tough. If you are truly God's son or daughter, He will never let you go. If you have walked down the path of sin, there are better, brighter days ahead of you. However, these words should also unsettle us because they contain a warning.

If God is truly concerned in finishing His work in us (and He is), how might we expect God to respond when we continue to run away from the life found in Him and toward sin?

While God is patient with us, He simply won't allow his children to continue down a road that will harm us. In His great love, He will come at us like a steam-roller to bring us back home to Him. One of the best evidences that you are a child of God is not that you never sin, but that you never continue in sin. Why? God promises us He simply won't allow it.

In the next personal study we will look at how God brings us back, but before we do that, let's consider how God has used our own realizations to shape our faith story.

Who needs to hear the story of how God has rescued you out of sin? When will you tell them?

End today by asking God to use your story to help someone who needs to hear it.

How God Brings Us Back

Think about the times in your life when you've received correction from a parent, friend, or teammate. What kind of correction do you find most helpful?

In the last personal study, we saw that God will always complete the work He begins in the lives of His sons and daughters. Throughout this study, we've seen the friction sin creates against God's work. Like anyone who cares for us, God will not let us persist in choices that are harmful. Because of His perfect care for us, He corrects us. Today we're going to look at the means God most often uses to call us back from the far off country. The first is the Holy Spirit.

The Leading of the Holy Spirit

Read John 16:7-8.

> **How is the Holy Spirit described here? What role does the Holy Spirit play in the life of a believer?**

> **How have you experienced the Holy Spirit's conviction concerning sin and righteousness?**

At the moment someone trusts in Jesus, the Holy Spirit comes to live inside of them. (See Rom. 8:11; 1 Cor. 3:16; Ezek 36:27.) The Bible calls this "indwelling" because the Spirit is dwelling inside of us, helping us resist the lies of the devil and the lure of sin.

Read John 16:13-14.

> **How does Jesus describe the work of the Holy Spirit in these verses? What is the ultimate goal of the Holy Spirit's work in our lives (v. 14)?**

Followers of Jesus never struggle against sin alone; we have help from the Spirit of God. When the devil assaults us with lies of a better life, the Holy Spirit urges us to remember our identity as children of God (Rom. 8:16). When our eyes are set on sin, He gently reminds us: "That's not who you are. You were not created for this. Turn around, and come back home." The Holy Spirit leads us to glorify God.

> **In what areas are you most tempted to find your identity outside of God?**

Most sin originates from a fundamental misunderstanding of who we are—sons and daughters of God. When we forget that identity, we live out of a false understanding of ourselves and pursue plans that can never fulfill us. In those times, God's Spirit prompts us to remember who we are in Jesus. But if we continue to resist the Spirit's urging, God will change tactics and remind us who we are by disciplining us as sons and daughters.

Disciplining Us as Sons and Daughters

This week we have seen that God is more committed to the work He began in our lives than we are. He desires for His children to continually become more and more like Jesus. Because of this desire, when we fall into sin God brings discipline to our lives which leaves us with no option but to come back home. God promises that He will discipline those He loves. And who does He love? He loves His sons and daughters.

Read Hebrews 12:5-8.

> **What is the difference between discipline and punishment? Why is it important to note that God disciplines us *because* we are sons and daughters?**

Like children who break free from their parents' hands and rush into parking lots, we lack the perspective to distinguish harmless fun from danger. We need correction. And like a good parent, God doesn't punish us; He disciplines to lead us down a better path.

> **How does discipline prove that we are children of God? Have you ever learned this by experience? If so, how?**

> **Based on this week of study, how will you respond differently the next time you sense the discipline of the Lord in your life?**

> **End your time together thanking God for the privilege of being His child. Thank the Spirit that Paul's words are true of you. Be sure to complete this week's four daily readings prior to the Week 6 meeting.**

For all who are being led by the Spirit of God, these are sons of God.
ROMANS 8:14

Romans 8:5-11

For the believer, the Holy Spirit is always at work in our lives to help us realize our sins and lead us in righteousness.

Read

Read the passage slowly and carefully with an open heart, asking the Holy Spirit to give you words of encouragement, direction, and correction.

Examine

Pick a few verses and look at them more closely to gain a deeper understanding of what the Bible is saying.

Apply

Consider how you will live differently in light of what you read.

- How aware are you of the Spirit's presence in your life?
- How might you develop a greater awareness of the Spirit's presence in your life?

Pray

Pray through the passage and your application, asking God to change your heart and to change your life based on the time you've spent in His Word.

Psalm 94:12-15

Notice how God uses discipline to guide His people back into a right relationship with Him.

Read

Read the passage slowly and carefully with an open heart, asking the Holy Spirit to give you words of encouragement, direction, and correction.

Examine

Pick a few verses and look at them more closely to gain a deeper understanding of what the Bible is saying.

Apply

Consider how you will live differently in light of what you read.

- What is one lesson you have learned from a time of discipline?
- What might God currently be teaching you through a frustrating situation or circumstance you are facing?

Pray

Pray through the passage and your application, asking God to change your heart and to change your life based on the time you've spent in His Word.

Acts 9:1-19

Saul persecuted the church with zeal until Jesus Christ confronted him on the road to Damascus. Saul realized the depth of his mistake and found the comfort of Jesus.

Read

Read the passage slowly and carefully with an open heart, asking the Holy Spirit to give you words of encouragement, direction, and correction.

Examine

Pick a few verses and look at them more closely to gain a deeper understanding of what the Bible is saying.

Apply

Consider how you will live differently in light of what you read.

- You may have never had an experience as dramatic as Paul's Damascus road experience, but you have felt and experienced God moving to change your perspective over the course of your life. Write about one such time below.

Pray

Pray through the passage and your application, asking God to change your heart and to change your life based on the time you've spent in His Word.

Proverbs 3:11-12

When God disciplines us, it is evidence of His love and grace and His desire for us to be reconciled to Him.

Read

Read the passage slowly and carefully with an open heart, asking the Holy Spirit to give you words of encouragement, direction, and correction.

Examine

Pick a few verses and look at them more closely to gain a deeper understanding of what the Bible is saying.

Apply

Consider how you will live differently in light of what you read.

- How can you make sure you don't despise God's instruction? What is one step you could take this week toward being more receptive to both God's instruction and the instruction of your parents and other spiritual leaders?

Pray

Pray through the passage and your application, asking God to change your heart and to change your life based on the time you've spent in His Word.

WEEK 6

The Speech

START

Welcome to Week 6. Use these questions to get the conversation started.

Last week we saw how the prodigal came to his senses after hitting rock bottom. Once you have come to your senses about a sinful decision you have made, what is the next step you should take?

In our time walking with the prodigal, we've seen the young man demand his inheritance and head for the promise of a better life in a far off country. We've heard how he wasted all his father's fortune and ended up wishing he ate as well as the pigs he tended to. Most recently, we saw the prodigal realize he'd made a big mistake and resolve to head back home to his father. This week, the prodigal wrestles with what he will say to his father when he returns.

What makes a good apology? What elements must be included?

On the other hand, how would you describe a bad apology?

Let's take a closer look at the speech the young prodigal prepared as he began his trek down the road home.

Ask someone to read Luke 15:18-19.

Pray and ask God to use our time together.
After praying, watch the video teaching.

WATCH

Use this section to take notes as you watch the Week 6 video.

DISCUSS

After viewing the video, discuss the following questions with your group.

Up until this point in the parable, we've only learned about the prodigal through what he has done. These verses mark a shift in the story. As the son rehearses what he will say when he faces his father, we're granted access into his heart. The first line is a blueprint for biblical repentance.

Verse 18 is the first line of the speech. What has the prodigal realized about himself and his father?

Why does true repentance require admitting our guilt to both God and others? Where do we see both in the prodigal's speech?

What are some excuses we make when we're wrong? What does making excuses do to our apologies?

The son says: "Father, I have sinned against heaven and before you" (Luke 15:18, ESV). He offers no excuses for his failure, nor does he try to claim his sin wasn't a big deal. Instead, he comes out and owns his sin against God and his father. True repentance involves a vertical aspect (admitting fault to God) and a horizontal aspect (admitting fault to the people our sin harmed).

Verse 19 is the second line of the speech. What is wrong with this statement? What has the son misunderstood about the love of his father?

When you seek God in forgiveness, what does your "speech" look more like—the first line, the second, or both? Explain.

Read Psalm 103:12.

Why is it important for us to realize that the depth of our sin can never be greater than the love of Jesus? Why do we need to know this not only when we mess up, but every day of our lives?

The prodigal's speech veered off the road when he said, "I am no longer worthy to be called your son" (Luke 15:19, ESV). We can never sin so much that God won't accept us. Nothing can ever separate us from the love of God in Jesus.

Model Repentance

When have you had to make a big apology? What elements did you include?

In our group study, we saw the speech the prodigal prepared on the way back to his father. You've probably had to come up with a similar speech at some point in your life—the one where you know you've done something wrong and the time has come to admit it. We all know the basic outline—"I've messed up really bad, and I hope that you will not give up on me." Sincere apologies take this shape because we all understand that true sorrow includes two elements—admitting fault and seeking restoration:

> *Father, I have sinned against heaven, and in your sight*
> **LUKE 15:18**

These are the words of a truly repentant person. He doesn't start his speech with excuses. He doesn't offer any deflection of his failure at all—he just comes out and owns his sin. These words are reminiscent of another key example of repentance.

Taking Ownership

Read Psalm 51:1-5.

How would you describe David's attitude? What lets us know that David is truly sorry as opposed to just being sorry that he got caught?

Earlier in this study we looked at David's sin with Bathsheba. Psalm 51 is David's response to this specific sin. David's prayer showed genuine sorrow and heartfelt repentance before God. David confronted his sin and didn't make excuses. He didn't deflect the blame onto others. He owned 100 percent of the responsibility. A person who is truly repentant owns their sins against God and others.

Do you find it harder to apologize to God or to others? Why are both necessary?

True repentance always has a horizontal aspect (realizing your sin against others) and a vertical one (realizing you have sinned against God). Realizing you've sinned against another person is important. Realizing you've sinned against the perfectly Holy God of the universe is even more important.

David acknowledged God as the primary party offended by his sin. Why is our sin always ultimately against God?

Besides truly owning his own sin, David also realized that, first and foremost, he sinned against God. This is significant considering all the people David had sinned against. The list is not short. He sinned against the nation of Israel by neglecting his kingly duties. He sinned against Bathsheba by lusting after her and calling his men to bring her to his room. He sinned against Uriah by taking his wife and then having him killed. Yet in all of these sins and in all of your sins, the most offended party is always God. He's God and He's the one who established the standard of holiness He calls us to live out.

Receiving Forgiveness

Read Psalm 51:6-12.

Once David admitted his sin, what changed about David's prayer?

What freedom have you found when you express your sin to God and others and ask for forgiveness?

Because God is the primary party offended by our sin, He is also the one with the power to restore and forgive us, which He will do every time. As he confesses guilt and asks for restoration, you can feel David's heart drawing closer to God. David's prayer transforms into a series of requests for restoration and renewal. Receiving forgiveness from God changes the way we live.

Embracing Restoration

Read Psalm 51:13-19.

How did David plan to live differently as a result of the forgiveness he received? Why should receiving forgiveness from God radically alter the way we live?

End today by thanking God for the forgiveness He's given you in Jesus. Use these words as a starting point:

Therefore there is now no condemnation for those who are in Christ Jesus.
ROMANS 8:1

The Radical Forgiveness of God

Have you ever sinned, failed, or messed up in a way that made you feel a palpable distance between you and God? It's common, because that's what sin does. It creates distance between us and God. While nothing can separate us from the love of God in Christ Jesus, our sin can create a sense of separation and make us question our relationship with God.

Have you ever felt distant from God? You probably have. What you need to know is that Satan loves to enter into the space created by the feeling of separation and fill it with lies. He will do everything he can to nurture and grow your doubts until you are too ashamed to approach God. Today, we're going to consider truth from Scripture that will help us combat this lie from the devil.

If We Confess Our Sins

Read 1 John 1:9.

> **Practically speaking, what does it mean to confess our sins? What does confession look like in the prodigal's speech in Luke 15:18?**

Confession is the role we play in regard to forgiveness. Confession is a word that means to "agree with." In other words, when we sin we agree with God that what we have done is wrong. The prodigal realized what he had done, agreed in his heart, and said with his mouth that he was wrong. The next part of the speech is where the prodigal—and we—miss the mark in understanding God's forgiveness.

> **Why should this verse give you confidence in approaching God for forgiveness?**

He is Faithful and Just to Forgive

> **Read the second line of the prodigal's speech in Luke 15:19 and then reread 1 John 1:9. What did the prodigal miss about the forgiveness of God?**

The amazing thing about God is that while we are often unfaithful, He is always faithful. It's impossible for God to be unfaithful to what He promises. We are like the prodigal; we believe we are unfit to be God's sons or daughters. Yet when we confess our sins, there will never be a time, place, or instance when sin will cause God to be unfaithful in offering His forgiveness to us.

Many of us simply don't believe God is faithful to forgive. We wonder deep down if there's a limit to His forgiveness. For example, when many of us mess up, we say a prayer like this: "God, I'm so sorry, please forgive me, please have mercy on me." From there we begin bargaining with God: "God, if you'll forgive me, I'll never do it again." When we do this, we are missing a crucial truth about God's character.

How do your own prayers reflect what you really believe about God's forgiveness? What kind of conditions do you tend to place on God forgiving you?

Notice that Scripture *doesn't* say that when we confess our sins, God is faithful and merciful to forgive us if we promise to never do it again. No, it says that God is faithful and just to forgive our sins.

What does it mean for someone to be "just"? What does it mean for God to be just in forgiving us?

God's justice in forgiving sin is a key concept that most of us simply haven't thought about in regard to God's forgiveness.

You see, when Christ came to this earth He lived a perfect life and never sinned. And when God sent Jesus to the cross, He did that so Jesus' shed blood would be the once-and-for-all payment for all of our sins. Not part of your sin. Not most of your sin. Not all of your sin except that really bad one you committed in high school. Jesus' blood is the only condition necessary for your forgiveness. When Jesus hung on the cross, battered, bleeding, and broken, He cried out, "It is finished!" If you are a Christian, your sin is finished; it was canceled by Jesus on the cross.

For God not to forgive you would be unjust. Why? Because all your sin was already paid for by Jesus. And for God not to forgive a sin that had already been paid for would be the height of injustice—something that God is incapable of. Your God is a faithful and just God. Your sin has already and forever been paid for, and His justice demands that He can never hold that sin against you. Now and forever.

Who do you know that struggles to believe God can really forgive them? What might it look like to help them see the depth of forgiveness using 1 John 1:9?

End your time by praying that God would give you the opportunity to share His forgiveness with someone this week. Don't forget to complete the four days of Bible readings before meeting with your group for Week 7.

REAP

Psalm 32:1-11

In addition to Psalm 51, this psalm highlights the blessing that comes from heartfelt repentance.

Read

Read the passage slowly and carefully with an open heart, asking the Holy Spirit to give you words of encouragement, direction, and correction.

Examine

Pick a few verses and look at them more closely to gain a deeper understanding of what the Bible is saying.

Apply

Consider how you will live differently in light of what you read.

- What is the connection between worship and confession?
- What might you need to confess to God this week in order to worship Him more deeply and more often?

Pray

Pray through the passage and your application, asking God to change your heart and to change your life based on the time you've spent in His Word.

1 John 1:5-10

This week we studied 1 John 1:9. Read this whole passage to develop a fuller appreciation of what John was writing.

Read

Read the passage slowly and carefully with an open heart, asking the Holy Spirit to give you words of encouragement, direction, and correction.

Examine

Pick a few verses and look at them more closely to gain a deeper understanding of what the Bible is saying.

Apply

Consider how you will live differently in light of what you read.

- How should knowing that God gave His Son on the cross for your sin change the way you approach Him in prayer?
- Write a prayer to God rooted in the confidence that comes from knowing you are His and you are forgiven.

Pray

Pray through the passage and your application, asking God to change your heart and to change your life based on the time you've spent in His Word.

Colossians 3:12-17

Once we have received radical forgiveness from God, it changes the way we live and interact with others.

Read

Read the passage slowly and carefully with an open heart, asking the Holy Spirit to give you words of encouragement, direction, and correction.

Examine

Pick a few verses and look at them more closely to gain a deeper understanding of what the Bible is saying.

Apply

Consider how you will live differently in light of what you read.

- What is one way you will seek to replace your sinful attitudes and actions with a Christlike perspective and Christlike actions?
- Is there someone at home or at school or at church that you need to forgive or seek forgiveness from? Pray for them now.

Pray

Pray through the passage and your application, asking God to change your heart and to change your life based on the time you've spent in His Word.

1 Timothy 1:15-16

Every sinner, without qualification, can receive forgiveness and live free from shame and guilt.

Read

Read the passage slowly and carefully with an open heart, asking the Holy Spirit to give you words of encouragement, direction, and correction.

Examine

Pick a few verses and look at them more closely to gain a deeper understanding of what the Bible is saying.

Apply

Consider how you will live differently in light of what you read.

- Take inventory: How has God been patient with you?
- Make a list: How will you let His love for you impact your love for others this week at home? at school? in your activities?

Pray

Pray through the passage and your application, asking God to change your heart and to change your life based on the time you've spent in His Word.

WEEK 7

The Return

START

- -

Welcome to Week 7. Use these questions to get the conversation started.

Is it sometimes difficult for you to believe that God can and will forgive you of your sin? Explain.

How does the truth of 1 John 1:9 help us fight the temptation of thinking that God's love for us is dependent on our behavior or spiritual performance?

How does knowing that God loves us no matter what motivate us to love and obey Him?

The prodigal has left home to find a far away land, wasted his inheritance, and found himself reeling from the devastation of his own selfish actions. He came to his senses and has prepared a speech to beg his father's forgiveness. He's on the way home.

This week, as the prodigal continues on the road home, we will deal with some of the barriers we build up in our hearts and minds that keep us from coming home to God. At home with the Father is the only place we are fully loved and accepted—free from guilt and shame.

Have you ever put off doing something that you needed to do for longer than you should? What kept you from moving forward?

Ask someone to read Luke 15:20.

Pray and ask God to use our time together.
After praying, watch the video teaching.

WATCH

Use this section to take notes as you watch the Week 7 video.

DISCUSS

After viewing the video, discuss the following questions with your group.

Notice how Jesus describes the prodigal's goal. Jesus could've said he arose and came home, or he could've said he arose and came to his hometown, but He didn't. Jesus said the prodigal "arose and came to his father" (Luke 15:20, ESV). That phrase is intentional. His father *was* home to him, just as for all children of God—our heavenly Father is home.

> **Do you see God as being "home" to you? Why is this a helpful way to view our relationship with the Father?**

For a child of God, no person or place in the entire world can ever be home except fellowship with God. But as Matt discussed in the video teaching, there are two barriers that keep children of God from going back home. The first is taking sin too seriously.

Why is it so easy to believe the lie that our sin is too great for God to overcome?

How might believing this lie hinder us from fighting sin?

Read Romans 5:20-21. How does realizing that God's grace is greater than our sin help us turn to our Father when we fall into sin?

The second barrier is that we do not take sin seriously enough.

Read Matthew 5:4. What does it mean to "mourn" your sin?

What is the difference between mourning your sin and taking it too seriously?

Read 2 Corinthians 5:21. How does the cross help us understand the cost of our sin?

How might taking time to mourn our sin keep us from being the kind of people who take repeated trips to the far off country?

Embrace the Love of God

As we pick up our story again, the prodigal's sin has left him devastated. He's prepared a speech to beg his father's forgiveness, and he's finally stepped out of the pigpen and taken those first steps to return home. In this week's personal studies, we will deal with two of the barriers that keep us from coming home to God and living with Him, unhindered by guilt and shame. We'll consider the first today.

If you're honest, do you ever struggle to believe God loves you? Why?

Doubting God's love for us often originates from a false belief that our sin is greater than God's love. Consider this example: you sin and step outside the bounds of God's best for your life, but instead of turning back to God you continue to rebel. You continue to wander farther from God, not because you want to continue sinning, but because you believe your failure has permanently damaged your relationship.

Thankfully, God is not like us; there will never be an uncorrectable breach in our relationship with Him because it's simply not possible to out sin God's love for us. God takes away our sin and uses all of our experiences—including our failures—to bring us closer to Himself.

How Can God Use Our Sin?

Read Romans 8:28-30.

Fill in the blank based on your reading: God causes _____ _____ to work together for good (Rom. 8:28).

To be clear, sin is always wrong, but it is never so severe that it will permanently damage your relationship with God. One of the fascinating things about God is He intentionally allows His children to struggle with certain parts of their walk with Him. Like a toddler learning to walk, progress takes time and multiple failures before growth occurs. The good news for you is that God is able to use "all things"—the good, the bad, and everything in between—for His glory.

Look at verses 28-30 again. What process does Paul outline for growth?

How have your failures led to a process of growth in your life?

In Romans 8, Paul said God has a plan for His children that never ceases. Paul says God has "predestined" or planned the lives of those who love Him (v. 29). As followers of Jesus, our entire life is a process where God makes us more like Jesus. No failure on our part can stop this work of God in our lives, because God's plan is not dependent on us. The plan begins with God before we are born and continues through our natural life until the time we enter into eternity (v. 30).

How have your failures caused you to grow in a way that your successes couldn't?

Think about it, if God made you perfect on the day you came to know Jesus, then you'd never again have to depend on Him. Instead of instant perfection, God allows us to have a journey of ups and downs, successes and failures, highs and lows, all with the intended design to keep us on a lifelong path of dependence on His grace. It's often in those seasons of hardship and struggle that God teaches us lessons that stick and make the greatest impact on our souls. And through those seasons of struggle and restoration, God shows us how He deals with our sin.

What Does God Do with Our Sin?

The Bible is filled with illustrations of how God deals with our sin.

Read the following verses: Psalm 103:12, Isaiah 38:17, Jeremiah 31:34, Micah 7:19, and Colossians 2:14.

If God doesn't remember our sins, why can't we stop thinking about them?

How does the cross help you see both the severity of your sin and also the depth of God's mercy and grace for you?

God has taken our sins as far away from us as possible. He took your sin, laid it upon Jesus, and expressed all of His judgment against sin on the cross. If you know Jesus, your sin is no problem for God. In fact, He chooses not to even remember it! You can never out sin God's love. He is always ready to receive those who return to Him.

End your time today by praying through the verses above, thanking God for fully removing your sin against Him. Commit to living in the forgiveness God has given you.

Mourn Your Sin

How would you describe your typical response to sin in your life? Grief, sorrow, indifference? Explain.

The Other Brother

While many of us struggle to accept the grace of God, many others swing to the opposite end of the spectrum—they fail to take their sin seriously enough. That's really what's going on with a character in the story of the prodigal son that we haven't talked about—the older brother. He's the brother who stayed home, stayed faithful, and kept working while his younger brother spent half of his inheritance on reckless living. When the younger brother finally came home (spoiler alert) and the father received him back, the older brother was furious. He thought to himself, "How can our father respond with grace after everything my younger brother has done?"

Read Luke 15:25-32.

How did the older brother respond to the celebration when his younger brother came home (v. 28)? Why did he respond this way?

When the older brother says this, what is he doing? He's comparing his sin to the younger brother's sin. And after he does the math, he thinks he deserves grace, but believes grace should be withheld from his younger brother. The Bible has a name for that attitude—it's called self-righteousness. And the crazy thing is that thinking too little of your sin can keep you from experiencing the fullness of the love of God in the same way that thinking too much of it can. So whether you think you've sinned too much to come back to God or you're more like the older brother, who didn't really think his sin was that bad, the Bible calls us to the same response.

The Right Response

Earlier in this study, we talked about the Beatitudes from the Sermon on the Mount. They are a list of attitudes and attributes that define a Christian. Here, Jesus outlined a proper response to sin. Jesus says:

Blessed are those who mourn, for they shall be comforted.
MATTHEW 5:4

How would you define the word "mourn"? Would you say that most people you know mourn their sin? Why or why not?

Jesus is showing us that there is blessing and a comfort that can only be found when we are emotionally disturbed by our sin. In the original language of the New Testament, the word Jesus uses for mourn goes beyond a common understanding of mourning. "Mourn" in Matthew 5:4 is a word that was most often used to describe the feelings associated with the loss of a loved one.

How closely does your view of sin line up with Jesus'? Does your sin bother you or cause you to mourn? Explain.

No sin is small or excusable. All sin needs to be taken seriously. When you lust after a person. When you respond with ungodly anger. When you assume the worst of someone who is different from you. When you won't forgive. When you pursue power and privilege for personal gain. When you cheat. When you lie. Fill in the blank—when you sin, the only way to truly mourn that sin is to look to the cross.

When you look to the cross, you'll see the only man who never sinned. And you'll see Him stripped naked, tortured, and beaten. You'll see nails that were driven through His hands and feet and a crown of thorns crushed into His brow. When you look to the cross, it will hit you that it was your sin that put Him there. Jesus Christ went through all of that because of you. And only then will you mourn.

Read 2 Corinthians 7:10. What does the Scripture say is the result of truly grieving our sins?

When God sees you sincerely mourning your sin, He will come to you, wrap His arms around you, and bless you with a comfort that can only be found in Him. According to Paul in the verse above, godly sorrow over sin leads to repentance. The word repentance means to do a 180-degree turn. It's not a one time apology, but rather, a choice to live differently. When we do this, Jesus says we will be happy. And not just your everyday run-of-the-mill kind of happy, but Jesus claims that we will experience the highest form of happiness available to us on this planet.

Read Psalm 139:23-24. Using these verses as a guide, ask God to help you mourn your sin so that you might look to Christ for the strength to live for Him. Be sure to complete the four Bible readings prior to the Week 8 group meeting.

Ephesians 1:1-10

Realize the magnitude of what God has accomplished on your behalf through the cross of Christ. Forgiveness and redemption are yours.

Read

Read the passage slowly and carefully with an open heart, asking the Holy Spirit to give you words of encouragement, direction, and correction.

Examine

Pick a few verses and look at them more closely to gain a deeper understanding of what the Bible is saying.

Apply

Consider how you will live differently in light of what you read.

- Paul said God has blessed every believer with every spiritual blessing in Christ (Eph. 1:3). Make a list of these spiritual blessings.
- Make a second list of how God has blessed you specifically.

Pray

Pray through the passage and your application, asking God to change your heart and to change your life based on the time you've spent in His Word.

Isaiah 61:1-4

Jesus quoted this verse at the beginning of His ministry. He came to give comfort to those who mourn their sin.

Read

Read the passage slowly and carefully with an open heart, asking the Holy Spirit to give you words of encouragement, direction, and correction.

Examine

Pick a few verses and look at them more closely to gain a deeper understanding of what the Bible is saying.

Apply

Consider how you will live differently in light of what you read.

- What has been troubling you lately? How might knowing that God promises comfort to those who mourn change your perspective?

Pray

Pray through the passage and your application, asking God to change your heart and to change your life based on the time you've spent in His Word.

Psalm 139:1-24

In order to realize where we have sin lurking in our hearts, it is imperative we ask God to search us and reveal to us hidden patterns of sin.

Read

Read the passage slowly and carefully with an open heart, asking the Holy Spirit to give you words of encouragement, direction, and correction.

Examine

Pick a few verses and look at them more closely to gain a deeper understanding of what the Bible is saying.

Apply

Consider how you will live differently in light of what you read.

- What is one thing about you that you try to hide from everyone else?
- Does it comfort you to know that God knows everything about you, including what you try to hide, and still loves you? Why or why not?

Pray

Pray through the passage and your application, asking God to change your heart and to change your life based on the time you've spent in His Word.

Mark 14:3-9

Realizing the grace we have received from Jesus brings a profound response like the one we see here in Mark's Gospel.

Read

Read the passage slowly and carefully with an open heart, asking the Holy Spirit to give you words of encouragement, direction, and correction.

Examine

Pick a few verses and look at them more closely to gain a deeper understanding of what the Bible is saying.

Apply

Consider how you will live differently in light of what you read.

- Take some time to honestly assess whether you are more like the woman in this story or the crowd who was upset with her. Write a prayer to God, asking Him to help you worship Him more passionately.

Pray

Pray through the passage and your application, asking God to change your heart and to change your life based on the time you've spent in His Word.

WEEK 8

The Reunion

START

Welcome to Week 8. Use these questions to get the conversation started.

Last week you were challenged to mourn your sin. How is this approach radically different from the way our culture typically responds to sin?

We've made it. The young man has finally completed his journey. He's rounding the last bend to the house, and he can see it now in the distance. The house, the front porch. The livestock grazing in the pastures that leads to his father's home. The familiarity of the scene no doubt gave him a sense of relief mixed with a wild uncertainty of what might unfold in the next few minutes. He looks again at his home growing closer by the second, and then he sees something he never could've expected. Still in the distance, waiting on the front porch, is his father. And what his father does next was almost impossible for the prodigal to believe.

Share about a time where you received grace that you didn't deserve.

Ask someone to read Luke 15:20-24.

Pray and ask God to use our time together.
After praying, watch the video teaching.

WATCH

Use this section to take notes as you watch the Week 8 video.

DISCUSS

After viewing the video, discuss the following questions with your group.

As the young man rounds the corner on the last stretch of his long walk home, he must have been wondering how his father would receive him. Would he be stern? enraged? disappointed? dismissive? Jesus subverts our expectations as the story concludes.

What is surprising about the father's reaction? How do you think the people who first heard this story would expect a father to act in this situation?

How would you expect the father to act?

Jesus seems to suggest the father saw the son in the distance because he was looking for him. What does this teach us about God?

Despite all the ways his son had wounded him, the father never stopped looking, straining his eyes toward the distance, hoping against hope that one day he would look up and see his son walking over the horizon. What Jesus is teaching us in this story is that we have a heavenly Father who never gives up on His kids.

Jesus teaches that God never gives up on us. If that's true, why are we so willing to believe He has?

Why is it important for us to realize that when we return to God we are celebrated, not shamed?

Matt ended his video teaching with an important question: Do you believe the best life is found at home with your heavenly Father? If so, how has the prodigal son helped solidify that truth in your heart? If not, what doubts remain?

What is your most important takeaway from our time studying the story of the prodigal son?

The God Who Won't Turn Away

Have you ever been tempted to think that you've messed up so badly or so frequently that God will throw up His hands and say "enough!"? If so, when?

Reading the story of the prodigal son, it's natural to wonder what the young man was thinking on that long walk home. No doubt, the prodigal spent a lot of time rehearsing his speech. He was probably beating himself up and wondering how his dad would respond, preparing for a worst-case scenario.

But what this wayward young man would soon discover is that every second of that long journey home he spent in fear and self-loathing were completely unfounded—for what was waiting for him was not a father who had written him off, but a father who loved so fiercely that it was beyond his ability to comprehend. Today we're going to look at the God who loves us this way.

God Is For Us

Read Romans 8:31-39.

What does it mean for God to be "for" us? When are you most tempted to believe that God isn't for you?

According to verses 32-34, what has God done to show that He is for us?

Like the prodigal's father, God is not waiting for us on the front porch, arms crossed, ready to rebuke us. At every moment, God is for you. When you are walking with Him or walking away from Him, God is for you. How can we know this? Paul says that God cares so much about you that He gave His own Son to free you from being bound to sin. The resurrection of Jesus Christ is proof that God's love for you is limitless.

Nothing Can Separate Us

In verse 35, Paul asks a series of rhetorical questions. What is the answer to all of these questions?

Look at verse 38-39. Write out a list of the things Paul claims are unable to separate us from the love of God in Jesus.

Of the things listed in Romans 8:35-39 that cannot separate believers from the love of Christ, which stands out to you the most? Why?

In this closing section of chapter 8, Paul asked one of the most important questions a person can ask: "Can anything separate me from the love of God?" (v. 35). Paul composed a list of threats we may perceive as separating us from God, arguing that none of these barriers could ever remove us from Christ's love for us. Nothing in all the world—no sin however awful—could ever separate you from Jesus. Every time we return to our Father, He will run to us, embrace us, and give us the best He has to offer.

If none of these things can separate us from Jesus, why do we sometimes believe the lie that we can somehow out sin God's love for us?

What evidence of God's love do you see in your daily life?

We live in a world where other people's love for us has limits. As humans, we have breaking points—imaginary lines drawn that if crossed mean another's love for us can diminish or even disappear. Some of you might have even experienced that horrible reality with a close friend, so it's difficult not to project that fear onto God when we have crossed a serious line. But Jesus is teaching us in this parable that God doesn't work that way. He's not like us. When it comes to His kids, there's no line we can cross where He says "enough." It's never going to happen. Are there consequences for our sin? Absolutely. But the consequences of sin will never result in God saying, "I'm done loving you."

God can no more stop loving you than He can stop being God. So while we are on our ridiculous trips to the far away land, He doesn't turn around and walk away in disgust—it's actually just the opposite. Jesus is showing us in this story, that at the moment of our rebellion, He turns His eyes to the horizon and won't stop watching and waiting for you until He sees your face.

End today by thanking God for the love He has shown you in Jesus. Receive His love, grace, and forgiveness anew.

The Searching God

We've spent the last eight weeks working through the story of the prodigal son, but the prodigal son is one of three parables in Luke 15. These stories were delivered in one address and each feature a lost object that is found and celebrated. Together they make one unified point—God's heart rejoices when a lost son or daughter comes back into relationship with Him. For our last personal study, let's take a look at these stories.

The God Who Finds

Read Luke 15:3-7.

How did the shepherd search for the sheep? What did he do when he found it?

The shepherd in this parable represents God. He found that one percent of his flock had gone missing, and he didn't write off the loss. Instead, he dropped what he was doing and poured his energy into finding the lost sheep. Once he found the sheep, he brought the sheep in close and threw a party. The search and the celebration far exceeded the perceived value of the lost sheep. Likewise, God rejoices when His lost sons and daughters are returned to His fold.

After the shepherd found the sheep, he took him back in. How can we welcome former prodigals back into the community of the church?

Next, Jesus tells the story of a woman looking for a lost coin.

The God Who Looks

Read Luke 15:8-10.

How is this parable similar to and different from the parable of the lost sheep?

What does the extensive search for such a seemingly insignificant object teach us about God's care for those who are lost or wandering?

This parable, like lost sheep and the prodigal son we've been studying for the last eight weeks, gives us a glimpse inside the heart of God. He is not content to sit and wait while one of His children is lost. He is the Shepherd who leaves the ninety-nine to search for the one. He is the woman who scours her house to find one coin. And He's the Father who is sitting with His eyes fixed on the horizon.

The God Who Runs

Read Luke 15:20-24.

When the father saw his son finally returning, his very first response was not to think to himself, "Well, there he is. It's about time that loser finally came to his senses!" The father didn't turn around and shout to the people in the house, "Hey, do you all remember my son? Yeah, the one who wasted my money. He's back. Let's see how this turns out." No. Those responses are how sinful people respond to other sinful people.

Jesus tells us that when the father finally saw the son, he hiked up his robe around his waist and took off in a dead sprint toward his son. This elderly, dignified father sprinted to embrace a son who had done nothing but show disdain for him and shame his family.

What does the running father reveal about the heart of God?

The son had come home. The father ran to him, embraced him, and clothed him with a robe and a ring. He ordered his servants to kill a fattened-calf and prepare for the party of the year. But before the party began, the father said one more thing.

Reread Luke 15:24.

With those final words of the father, Jesus is teaching us one final lesson. It's a benediction of sorts that sums up and ties a bow on everything He hoped we'd learn from the story. In a way, this is Jesus' thesis statement—one sentence that encapsulates the grand lesson of the entire parable. The father said, "This son of mine was dead and has come to life again." With those words, Jesus is making a bold and final claim. The far away land of sin = death. At home with the Father = life.

End your time today praying God would reassure you of His love for you. Don't forget to complete the four days of daily readings.

REAP

Luke 15:11-32

Stories like the prodigal son deserve return visits. Read this story one last time and see what you notice that you hadn't noticed before.

Read

Read the passage slowly and carefully with an open heart, asking the Holy Spirit to give you words of encouragement, direction, and correction.

Examine

Pick a few verses and look at them more closely to gain a deeper understanding of what the Bible is saying.

Apply

Consider how you will live differently in light of what you read.

- What details or verses stood out to you during your final read of the parable of the prodigal son?
- How are you going to live differently after studying and learning from the prodigal son for the last eight weeks?

Pray

Pray through the passage and your application, asking God to change your heart and to change your life based on the time you've spent in His Word.

Luke 17:1-4

Knowing Jesus should lead us to enthusiastically embrace and restore those who seek forgiveness.

Read

Read the passage slowly and carefully with an open heart, asking the Holy Spirit to give you words of encouragement, direction, and correction.

Examine

Pick a few verses and look at them more closely to gain a deeper understanding of what the Bible is saying.

Apply

Consider how you will live differently in light of what you read.

- How might you be acting as a stumbling block for others? What will you do to change this?
- Who in your life might be a stumbling block leading you further into sin? What changes do you need to make to be on your guard?

Pray

Pray through the passage and your application, asking God to change your heart and to change your life based on the time you've spent in His Word.

Romans 12:1-21

The father in the prodigal acts in a countercultural way. As followers of Jesus, we embrace this countercultural love and grace as a lifestyle.

Read

Read the passage slowly and carefully with an open heart, asking the Holy Spirit to give you words of encouragement, direction, and correction.

Examine

Pick a few verses and look at them more closely to gain a deeper understanding of what the Bible is saying.

Apply

Consider how you will live differently in light of what you read.

- Read the list of gifts in verses 6-7 again. Prayerfully consider which of these may be your gifting, and jot down a few ways you can use your gifting in your church and community.

Pray

Pray through the passage and your application, asking God to change your heart and to change your life based on the time you've spent in His Word.

2 Corinthians 5:18-21

Our Father calls us to go into all the world and tell all who will listen how to find the reconciliation we've found as members of His family.

Read

Read the passage slowly and carefully with an open heart, asking the Holy Spirit to give you words of encouragement, direction, and correction.

Examine

Pick a few verses and look at them more closely to gain a deeper understanding of what the Bible is saying.

Apply

Consider how you will live differently in light of what you read.

- How can you share all you have learned about God's love for His sons and daughters with your friends and neighbors this week? Make it a point to share with those who do not believe they can be forgiven or who have never accepted God as their Father.

Pray

Pray through the passage and your application, asking God to change your heart and to change your life based on the time you've spent in His Word.

Leader Guide

How to Use This Leader Guide

Prepare to Lead

Before each session, go over the video teaching and read through the group discussion to prepare for the group meeting.

Familiarize yourself with the questions and begin thinking about how to best utilize these questions for the group you are leading. The following sections of the leader guide are given to help you lead students well.

Main Point

This section summarizes the big idea of each session. Use this section to help focus your preparation and leadership during the group session.

Key Scriptures

Key passages of Scripture are listed for quick reference.

Considerations

The purpose of leading a group is to bring God's Word to the people in the group. This section is designed to help you consider and wrestle with the ideas in each session and to suggest ways to apply those truths to your group.

Pray

Use the prayer provided to close the group session.

Week 1

The Problem

Main Point

This first session introduces us to the parable of the prodigal son and the crucial question at the center of the study. More than ever before, people are asking the question, "If I go all-in with living out my Christian faith, am I missing out on the best that life has to offer?" The prodigal asked it, and many of the people around us are asking the same question today.

Key Scriptures

- Luke 15:11-24
- Matthew 13:44

Considerations

Though this story may be familiar to many, there may be students in your group who have never heard it. Matt goes over the parable in the video teaching, but be sure to have someone read the Scripture slowly and clearly to get everyone on the same page at the beginning.

Also, be mindful that there may be students in your group asking the same question the prodigal did. Be aware and prayerful that God will answer their questions through this study.

Pray

Ask God to give you and your group the grace to hear Him clearly through this story Jesus told. Pray for wisdom and understanding. Confess your belief in the Bible as God's inspired Word. Ask the Spirit to use the Scriptures and our time together to teach, rebuke, and correct us over these next eight weeks.

_____

_____

_____

_____

_____

_____

_____

_____

Week 2

The Lie

Main Point

This session builds upon the last session and focuses on the lie that led the prodigal to wander from home—the false belief that true life is found in the far off country. If life with God is so good and satisfying, why in the world are we tempted to leave Him for what we think are greener pastures? Matt gives two answers:

1. Our sinful flesh
2. The lies of the devil

Key Scriptures

- Luke 15:11-12
- John 8:44

Considerations

All sinful thoughts and actions are rooted in false beliefs. This section asks us to consider our beliefs in light of the choices we make. There are likely students in your group who have never thought about their actions this way. This session should lead us to ask what lies of the devil have we believed that are keeping us from God's best for our life.

Pray

Praise the Lord Jesus Christ that His power has overwhelmed the devil, hell, and the grave. Ask the Spirit to guide us into truth and to resist the lies of the devil. Pray that the Spirit will give us the armor of God and provide us with discernment and understanding to see the lies of the devil and trust God.

Week 3
The Step

Main Point

Jesus told the story of the prodigal son so we could see his mistakes and avoid making similar ones ourselves. All sin begins with a first step. The key to this session is understanding the difference between temptation and sin and knowing how to cut temptation off before it becomes sin, because sin never ends well.

Key Scriptures

- 2 Samuel 11:1-14 (Chapters 11–12 for broader context)
- James 1:14-15

Considerations

You'll want to be aware that some students in your group may have recently given into temptation. If so, they may be raw or sensitive about the content from this session. No matter where students are in their walk with God, we want to point out the negative consequences of sin in light of the glory of God.

Pray

Ask God that by His Spirit's power, we will be people who flee from sin and run back to Him. For those of us considering sin at this moment, ask that we will see the escape from temptation that God has provided and have the courage to take it. Give thanks to God for delivering us.

_____

_____

_____

_____

_____

_____

_____

Week 4
The Consequences

Main Point

In this session, we see the prodigal feel the weight of his sin. Instead of feasting at his father's table, he hungers for the pods the pigs are eating. This part of the parable clarifies a crucial truth—sin always has consequences.

Key Scriptures
- Luke 15:13-16
- Ecclesiastes 3:11

Considerations

Many teens, even those who are Christians, think of sin as something that's "not a big deal." Help lead your students to a more biblical view of sin and its consequences. The point is to help students see that sin is both a big deal and that there is a better way.

If students are feeling empty, point them back to God. That emptiness they feel is God asking them to wake up. Sin never satisfies; God always does.

Pray

Thank God for placing eternity in our hearts in order that we may seek and find Him. Thank the Spirit for allowing us to feel the consequences and weight of our sin. Pray for the students in your group who are feeling the weight of their own sin—that they will find their comfort in Jesus and receive His forgiveness.

_____

_____

_____

_____

_____

_____

Week 5
The Realization

Main Point

Sin, for the believer, is a monumental waste of time. God cares so much about His work in our lives that He will not allow us to stay in sin. He always brings us back through discipline or through the leading of the Holy Spirit.

Key Scriptures

- Luke 15:17
- Philippians 1:6
- John 16:7-8

Considerations

Pay particular attention to the two people Matt addresses at the end of the video teaching—those considering sin and those stuck in a pattern of sin. With empathy and understanding, do your part to help students recognize this and find their way out.

Pray

Praise God that He brings conviction and discipline in our lives that we may turn back to Him. Ask Him to bring that conviction where sin is present among students tonight. Pray that your group might be a place where students can wrestle against sin and find encouragement and comfort in their struggles.

Week 6
The Speech

Main Point

This session takes us inside the speech the prodigal was preparing to deliver to his father. Through this we see two crucial truths. First, true repentance is unqualified acknowledgment of sin against God coupled with a desire to be right with God and others who have been harmed by our sin. But the second part of the speech reveals a flaw in the son's thinking—he believed he had out sinned his father's love. We see in this session that it is not possible for our sin to outweigh God's love for us.

Key Scriptures

- Luke 15:18-19
- Psalm 51:2-4

Considerations

You will want to help students see two things.

First, their sin is always first and foremost against God.

Second, you will want to help those who feel like their sin makes them irredeemable. Even for Christians, it is common to believe that we have sinned so grievously that God will no longer accept us. This is simply not true, but breaking the hold of this lie may require time and patience. Your role as a leader is to help students see this beautiful truth and begin to take it to heart.

Pray

Pray that we will always be repentant people. Praise God that when we seek forgiveness, He always gives it. Ask Him to restore relationships broken by sin and press into our souls the reality that we can never go so far from Him that we can't return.

_____

_____

_____

_____

_____

_____

_____

Week 7
The Return

Main Point

This week we see the prodigal continuing his journey home. Through this section of the parable we see two barriers that keep us from coming home to God: 1) We take our sin too seriously and believe our sin is greater than God's love for us, or 2) we don't take sin seriously enough and believe our sin is a minor bump in the road that we shouldn't mourn or repent of.

Key Scriptures

- Luke 15:20
- Romans 5:20-21
- Matthew 5:4
- 2 Corinthians 5:21

Considerations

You likely have students in your group who take sin too seriously and not seriously enough. Make sure to devote equal time to each and help students realize the errors of both types of thinking.

Encourage everyone to be open and honest about which error they lean toward.

Pray

Pray that God will give us the wisdom to see if we are taking sin too seriously or not seriously enough. Thank Him that He will always receive those who come to Him in repentance and faith and commit to live in light of His love toward us.

_____

_____

_____

_____

_____

Week 8
The Reunion

Main Point

This last session is the key to understanding the whole story. When we mess up—when we take off to the far off country of sin—God is not waiting for us with His arms crossed, face covered in disappointment, ready to discipline. He is the Father who runs to us ready to receive and restore us into a full relationship as His son or daughter.

Key Scriptures

- Luke 15:20-24

Considerations

Closing the study is an ideal time to reflect on how far we've come. Be sure to remind students of the story and give time to discuss key takeaways from our time studying this parable together.

Encourage those who still may be wrestling with sin to return to their Father, who is ready and willing to receive them.

Pray

Thank God for the truth that is revealed to us through His Son and through this story in the Scriptures. Praise God that no matter how far we wander, we can always return to our home with Him.

Notes